X

Mary McLeod Bethune

Mary McLeod Bethune

By Rinna Evelyn Wolfe

Franklin Watts
New York London Toronto Sydney
A First Book

I would like to thank Anne Rice and Crystal Porter for special materials, Joel Vinson for testing the recipe, and Frances Whitney for her constant support. And I am indebted to Mrs. Helen Williams-Bronson of Bethune-Cookman College, Mrs. Dorothy Stephans-Hogan, Dr. P. Rogers Fair, Sr., and the late Edward Rodriquez for personal stories, which made Mrs. Bethune come alive again.

Rinna Wolfe

Cover photograph copyright ©: New York Public Library, Picture Collection
Photographs copyright ©: New York Public Library, Schomburg Center for Research in Black Culture: pp. 2, 18, 20; North Wind Picture Archive: pp. 12, 14, 40; The Moody Bible Institute: p. 22; Art Resource, N.Y./D. Donne Bryant: p. 26; Bethune Cookman College: pp. 28, 29, 32, 35 bottom, 47, 49; New York Public Library, Picture Collection: p. 35 top; The Library of Congress: pp. 37, 43; UPI/Bettmann Newsphotos: pp. 53, 55; Photri Inc./Tamara K. Liller: p. 57.

Library of Congress Cataloging-in-Publication Data

Wolfe, Rinna.
Mary McLeod Bethune / by Rinna Evelyn Wolfe.
p.   cm.—(A First book)
Includes bibliographical references (p.   ) and index.
Summary: A biography of the black educator who sought equality for members of her race.
ISBN 0-531-20103-1
1. Bethune, Mary McLeod, 1875–1955—Juvenile literature.   2. Afro-Americans—Biography—Juvenile literature.   3. Teachers—United States—Biography—Juvenile literature.   [1. Bethune, Mary McLeod, 1875–1955.   2. Teachers.   3. Afro-Americans—Biography.]   I. Title. II. Series.
E185.97.B34W65   1992
370′.92—dc20
[B]   91-31660 CIP AC

CONTENTS

INTRODUCTION

Eight-year-old Mary McLeod stood with her father Samuel at Marse Eli's *cotton gin* on a fall day in 1883. She watched as men packed down loose cotton and wrapped it with metal bands, then raised the *bale* and moved it along a numbered line. "You've got two hundred and fifty pounds there, Sam," Marse Eli said.

"Isn't it four hundred eighty pounds?" Mary asked softly.

Surprised, Marse Eli looked again. "I believe you're right, Mary. You're a smart girl," he said. That day, perhaps for the first time, Mary's father received an honest price for his cotton crop.

Mary was the only McLeod who could read, write, add, and subtract. Eventually she taught her father how to figure numbers and helped neighbors—both black and white—to keep accurate records. "From the first," she said, "I made learning, what little it was, useful in every way I could."

Mary McLeod Bethune became an educator, organizer, and political leader long before America's Civil Rights Movement began. The programs she started helped ensure human rights for millions of people around the globe.

1 COTTON-PICKING DAYS

Mary Jane, the fifteenth child of seventeen, was born on July 10, 1875, in Mayesville, South Carolina. Looking into her new daughter's open eyes, Patsy McLeod, an ex-slave, thought, "She will show us the way out."

Neither Patsy nor Mary's father, Samuel, had a *surname* until Samuel chose McLeod, his ex-master's family name.

Tall and muscular, Samuel was a kind, skillful carpenter and farmer, who also worked well with leather and tin. Patsy cooked nearby in the big McIntosh house. Small and *lithe*, she walked with the queenly grace of her royal African ancestors. Her smile lit Samuel's heart.

When Samuel asked McLeod for permission to marry Patsy, his master agreed. But first Samuel had to earn the money to buy her. So after doing a normal day's work, he labored for other farmers, and, in two years, the loving couple celebrated their wedding.

Since Samuel and Patsy were considered property, they had no rights. They had to stand by and watch most of their children be traded to local slaveowners. Through the *Underground*, however, they kept in touch with them, and they all reunited after the Civil War ended in 1865.

For the next decade, they lived on their ex-master's land. Samuel farmed and Patsy did laundry. They saved her wages to buy five acres of uncultivated, hilly soil. Together they and their grown sons later purchased thirty additional acres.

Samuel and his oldest sons built a three-room log cabin near the tallest oak tree on their property. The house had a wooden door, two wooden shutters, a brick chimney, and a fireplace. Samuel soon added a front porch, a rear kitchen with a brick oven, and a shed behind the house where everyone washed in a communal *trough*. Patsy named the cabin The Homestead.

Samuel attached shelves to the walls one above the other in the two side rooms. There the children slept on mattresses Patsy sewed and filled with dried moss. The family shared the middle room, which they called The Hall.

Samuel and the boys fished in a stream and caught quail, possum, and rabbits in the woods. The children collected apples and peaches in vacated orchards and dried and stored the fruit for winter.

Thrifty and practical, Patsy planted vegetables, a fig

tree, a grapevine, and flowers. She liked to say, "I can sit under my vines . . . enjoy peaches and cream. And none shall make [us] afraid." The McLeods treasured their independence.

Mary's older siblings lived elsewhere with families of their own. The seven at home rose before dawn to do chores. They hitched up the mule, Old Bush, and led the cow to pasture. They made beds and washed dishes, taking special care of Patsy's chipped china and glasses, gifts from her ex-mistress.

After a breakfast of hominy *grits*, bacon fat, and coffee, everyone except fragile Grandmother Sophia headed barefoot for the fields.

A good cotton crop supported the family. It brought in enough dollars to pay debts, buy *staples*, and leave something over for extras. Through spring and summer, everyone spread fertilizer, planted seeds, battled crabgrass, chopped weeds, and watched ripening red flowers become full-blown cotton bolls. When the white fluff bloomed in fields everywhere, they picked cotton at a furious speed.

When Mary was five, she sat atop Old Bush, guiding him through straight furrows. Four years later she was picking 250 pounds of cotton a day!

After supper, Mary and her brothers and sisters wiped mud from farm tools, oiled the leather harness to prevent cracking, and filled lamps with kerosene.

On chilly nights the family sat close to the fireplace.

Picking cotton was strenuous, backbreaking work. Farmers labored all year long to produce a plentiful crop.

In her rocker, smoking a long-stemmed pipe, Grandmother Sophia told Bible stories and tales about Africa and slavery. At her grandmother's knee, Mary learned African customs and songs in a language she did not understand. She grew proud of her African heritage.

The McLeods began and closed every day with prayers. On Sundays they attended church in Mayesville.

Before bedtime every night, Samuel led a hymn. Mary loved these hours together.

Neighbors gathered at The Homestead's oak tree to hear a traveling minister's sermon, to pray, and to sing together. Mary, who inherited her father's sweet voice, especially loved the old slave songs and hymns, such as "Nearer My God to Thee."

Most ex-slaves were sharecroppers who traded labor and a portion of the crops they grew for tools, fertilizer, and seed from the owner of the land. The McLeods, however, were independent landowners, and the community relied on their leadership. Samuel helped other farmers. Patsy often delivered babies and used the herbs she grew to cure the sick. Watching her mother give food to the needy from their precious stores, Mary learned early to help anyone who knocked at the door.

Difficult as farming was, people often enjoyed themselves. Poor blacks and poor whites ate and danced at each other's parties, at cotton pickings, corn *huskings*, and sugarcane *taffy* pulls. Sometimes, when they felt sorry for an unskilled former master who had fallen on hard times, they helped him out. Then they stayed on for supper.

The Fourth of July was a gala day for the McLeods. Parents, children, and grandchildren celebrated not only the country's independence, but their own freedom as well. It also became party-day for their July-born children, Mary and her oldest and youngest sisters.

Once, a day after Mary's birthday, her father took her

Sharecroppers bought their supplies on credit, and exchanged a portion of their crop for use of the land. Usually these costs kept them in debt to the landowners for years.

to a horse show in Mayesville. Suddenly a drunken white man in the crowd shoved a flaming match close to a black man's face. "Blow it out!" he commanded.

The black man tried to ignore him. But when he shouted again, the black man pushed him to the ground.

Samuel hurried Mary away but not before she heard white men yelling for a *lynching*. Under her quilt that night she heard echoes of their rage in her ears.

Weekly, Patsy washed and ironed for white folks, to earn a few extra pennies. One Saturday Mary waited outside a large house while her mother delivered the fresh linen. Two of the owner's grandchildren invited her to play with them. But when Mary reached past their dolls for a book, one of the girls said sharply, "Put that down. *You* can't read!"

Upset and confused, Mary wondered why white people acted so mean to black people. She determined to educate herself.

Mary was too young to understand how the South was changing. In the 1880s, free black children had no schools near Mayesville. Slaves had been forbidden to read or write, and after the Civil War 90 percent of all black people were *illiterate*. Southerners tried to keep them unschooled. They feared that educated blacks would demand schools, better houses, and jobs with higher pay, and that they would lose control.

Mary could not know that soon a stranger would come to change her life.

2 MARY'S WORLD EXPANDS

In 1882, city-dressed, light-skinned Miss Emma Wilson knocked at The Homestead door. Mary had never before heard a black woman called "Miss." She was impressed. Miss Wilson was seeking black children for her new mission school in Mayesville. The McLeods agreed to send Mary.

One October day, carrying a new *slate* and lunch pail, wearing a thin shawl over a gingham dress, seven-year-old Mary hiked in heavy, metal-toed shoes the five miles to town. In the afternoon she would walk the five miles back. In a tiny shack she learned reading, writing, the magic of numbers, new games, and songs.

The second year, the "Mayesville Institute" moved into a two-room brick building. Pupils sat at rickety desks. Miss Wilson wrote on chipped cardboard painted black, and the children's drawings and paper flowers decorated the walls. Mary never missed a class, and nightly after supper, she taught her family everything she learned.

Mary was an efficient organizer. She knew her parents hid money in safe places because it was unlawful for blacks to deal with banks. Once she understood math, she convinced friends to do without candy, and instead to save the pennies they earned selling berries. Then, acting as banker, she started the Tin Can Banking Circle. Come Christmas, the children had enough money to give their families store-bought presents.

When Mary was eleven, Patsy and Samuel proudly watched their daughter graduate in Mayesville's first class of black students. Mary yearned for more schooling, but the family's mule had died and had to be replaced. Money was scarce now, so she put away her ribbon-tied diploma and returned to the cotton fields.

A year later, Miss Wilson brought news that would further widen Mary's world. A white Quaker dressmaker in Denver, Colorado, Miss Mary Crissman, had offered to pay tuition for one worthy student at Scotia Seminary, Miss Wilson's alma mater. Miss Wilson chose Mary for the award.

Mary's good fortune excited the entire community. People gave her knitted stockings, crocheted collars, and used clothes which Patsy altered to fit her. On departure day people stopped work and rode mules and wagons, or walked to the railroad station. They watched proudly as the

*Mary always encouraged youngsters
to learn skills, become educated,
and lead lives of service.*

train carried their brightest twelve-year-old 150 miles from home. Waving good-bye, they sang the encouraging song "Climbing Jacob's Ladder."

Eight hours later a white teacher welcomed a sooty Mary to Concord, North Carolina. Scotia Seminary's grandeur overwhelmed Mary: two-story buildings with glass windows and wide stairs—Mary had never climbed a stairway! A room to share with just one girl, a bed with sheets, a bureau and a desk of her own, a rose-patterned washbasin—all were luxuries no one had at home!

Mary ate meals with three hundred pupils at tables laid with white cloths, knives, forks, and spoons. She marveled that black and white teachers not only worked together, but ate together as well.

Mary's smile, wit, and dramatic flair attracted friends. Although she was an average student, she wrote good compositions in poor handwriting. She enjoyed history, geography, and Latin, and struggled through algebra and geometry. She excelled in music and sang in the choir. Years later she wrote: "The white teachers taught that the color of a person's skin has nothing to do with his brains — and color, caste or class distinctions are evil. . . ."

Miss Crissman paid her tuition, but Mary earned room and board by gardening, dusting, cooking, and sometimes ironing her principal's shirts. Summers she babysat or cleaned white families' houses. Twice, she saved enough to visit her parents. At home, she showed neighbors how to trim a hat and invent new hairstyles.

*Years after graduating from Scotia Seminary,
Mary still remembered the ideas of equality
set forth by the white teachers. Her early
education helped prepare her to battle
for equal rights throughout her life.*

At Scotia, Mary heard religious missionaries talk about saving African "savages." Were these the same people whose beautiful songs and legends Grandmother Sophia had talked about? Mary decided she would serve God in Africa. So before graduation, she applied to Moody Bible Institute in Chicago, Illinois, for training. When she was accepted, Miss Crissman again paid the tuition.

Barely nineteen, in July 1894, a poised Mary arrived in Chicago, a city that had sheltered runaway slaves before the Civil War. She moved about with ease in this metropolis of stockyards, factories, office buildings, and streetcars. Although she was the only "Negro" among the one thousand Moody students, here she felt she gained "a love for the whole human family."

At Moody, Mary was sent to work among the poor. She sang on street corners and in local jails. She fed the homeless, visited people in *tenements*, and helped start Sunday schools outside of Chicago.

One day she knocked at an apartment door and walked into a room filled with drinking men and women. Someone locked the door. Sitting quietly, she endured jeers and jokes until one woman persuaded the crowd to let her go.

"I wasn't afraid," she said. "I knew I had protection."

In 1896, Mary applied to the Presbyterian Mission

Top: Here, Mary McLeod poses with her class at Moody Bible Institute. She is seated in the third row, sixth from the left. Right: After leaving Moody, Mary was disappointed when she could not become a missionary in Africa. But without knowing it, she would soon start on her life's work— teaching in America.

Board for a missionary job in Africa. Its members said Africa had "no openings for Negroes." Bitterly disappointed, she returned home to teach with Emma Wilson.

The following year she took a position teaching eighth grade at the Haines Institute in Augusta, Georgia. Lucy Croft Laney, a former slave, had made this small school a "torchlight" of learning in the African-American community. Here Mary realized that her life work lay in America among her own people.

Lucy Laney taught Mary how to make every experience a lesson. After a week of teaching, on Sunday mornings Mary and her students entered nearby *shanties* to distribute clothes, soap, towels, toothbrushes, and combs, and to bathe and feed children. In the afternoons, Mary taught Bible class and hymns. Before long, city social workers joined her as volunteer teachers.

The following year, Mary moved to Sumter, South Carolina, to teach at Kindell Institute. Living on a tight budget, she sent most of her wages home. A fire had destroyed The Homestead, and her salary helped pay a new mortgage and support two sisters at Scotia. (Years later, Mary bought her parents a small, comfortable house with glass windows.)

While in Sumter, Mary met Albertus Bethune, a handsome tenor in the church choir. He, too, was a teacher. In 1898, when their friendship turned to love, they married and moved to Savannah, Georgia. Their only child, Albert McLeod Bethune, was born on February 3, 1899.

Restless at home, Mary accepted a teaching post in a new mission school in Palatka, Florida. To increase their income, Albertus became a menswear salesman and Mary worked part-time for the Afro-American Insurance Company.

Every day, Mary met families heading for Florida's east coast. The men expected to help build a new railroad to Miami's luxury hotels and beaches. Who would teach their children, she wondered.

One night Mary dreamed she was trying to cross the St. Johns River. But there was neither boat nor bridge in sight. Suddenly a man's voice said, "Look ahead of you." On turning, Mary saw thousands of boys and girls in uniforms coming toward her. Handing her a pencil, the man commanded, "Write down every name."

For years Mary had thought about "somedays." Someday life would be better. Someday she would teach boys, girls, men, and women skills in her own school. On awakening, she realized she had to start that school now!

3 "ENTER TO LEARN. DEPART TO SERVE."

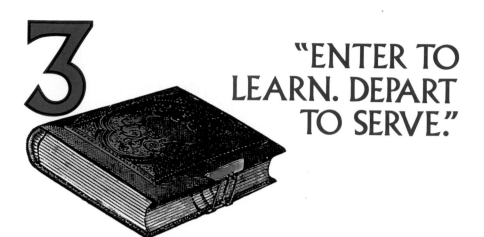

Albertus was not enthusiastic about Mary's vision. How could she start a school? She didn't have any money.

Consequently, Mary set out for Daytona Beach alone with five-year-old Albert. They traveled by train in a "*Jim Crow*" car. The strictly enforced Jim Crow laws separated blacks from whites in public places—schools, churches, restaurants, hospitals, public facilities, and neighborhoods.

Mary arrived with a dollar and a half in her purse. She strolled along unpaved streets where African-Americans lived in shabby houses without running water. Closer to the hills and river, whites lived in stately homes amid towering trees.

Wealthy white women, members of the Palmetto Club, had opened a kindergarten for their servant's children. But without question, "Colored Town" needed its own school.

Old slave houses such as the one pictured here were still used by some poor blacks long after the Civil War had ended.

Mary moved in temporarily with Mrs. Susie Warren and went house-hunting. But neighbors worried. The Ku Klux Klan, organized after the Civil War, was committing brutal, lawless acts against black people and could cause trouble for a "colored" school.

Unafraid, Mary found a two-story house shaded by tall palms and oaks on a dirt road. The roof leaked and the front steps sagged. The inside needed repairs but it had a well and a toilet in the yard. Mary and Albert could live upstairs. Classes would be held below.

The owner, John H. Williams, wanted eleven dollars a month rent. But Mary convinced him to take a fifty-cent deposit and trust her for the rest.

With borrowed broom and rags, she scrubbed and polished. She salvaged cracked dishes and broken furniture from the dump and garbage piles behind hotels. "Creating something from nothing," as she said, she made charcoal pencils from burnt logs and ink from elderberry juice. She used crates for chairs and a large packing case for her desk. Like her mother, she made mats of corn sacks filled with Spanish moss.

Once a week, she bicycled door-to-door begging cash donations. She told everyone her pupils would learn to use "their heads to think, their hands to work and their hearts to have faith." Mary's faith never wavered.

Despite their fears, people gave a chair, a frying pan, a washtub. Women shared food and sold chicken dinners to raise funds. After Mary read a letter for an illiterate

woman, the woman gave her an old cookstove. Fishermen brought fish. Orange growers contributed bruised fruit. The local grocer gave Mary sweet potatoes and eggs on credit, with which she baked and then sold steaming sweet potato pies to railroad crews.

On October 4, 1904, Mrs. Bethune opened the Daytona Literary and Industrial School for Training Negro Girls with three Warren girls—Lucille, Ruth, and Lena—and Anna Geiger, Celeste Jackson, and her own son. She

*Washing clothes was one of the many chores
at Daytona the children were taught to do.*

prayed for them to "Enter to learn. Depart to serve," words
which became the school creed. Tuition was fifty cents a
week, but she turned no child away.

Along with the ABCs, Mrs. Bethune taught home-
making and crafts. Sensing that adults also wanted to learn
to read and write, she soon started evening classes. Besides

the basics, she taught budgeting and child care, and emphasized prayer. Grown-up pupils either paid a dollar a week or helped repair the house.

When parents had to travel with employers, their children boarded at the school. Within two years, Mrs. Bethune added volunteer teachers and rented a second building for her nearly two hundred youngsters, which included a few boys.

Overseer of everything, she wrote and distributed leaflets, sought donations, paid bills, and mothered the children. Money was always scarce. Yet, miraculously, whenever they needed food, it arrived. Sometimes railroad men or trusted prisoners from a nearby prison left provisions. Occasionally, her adult students each contributed a dollar to pay an outstanding grocery bill.

Sunday afternoons Mrs. Bethune welcomed everyone to a three o'clock meeting. At first only African-Americans came to her talks about black history and to sing spirituals and hymns. But after a friend donated a foot-pedal organ, clever coachmen drove their rich employers past the school. Drawn to the music, they too stepped inside. Ignoring *segregation* laws, Mrs. Bethune shook their hands, chatted, and invited them to sit anywhere. She believed these winter tourists could become allies, and she was right. In time, the house was packed.

Eventually Albertus joined her in Daytona. He drove a horse-and-buggy taxi and helped out in the school. After his son transferred to Haines Institute, Albertus accepted a position in a boys' school in Savannah, Georgia. He died of tuberculosis in 1919.

Mrs. Bethune trained her girls to sing. She then arranged for concerts in churches and in big hotels, to acquaint people with her program. Audiences everywhere were impressed, and she never left empty-handed. The industrialist John D. Rockefeller became a fan and later provided generous grants and scholarships for the school.

Frugal as Mrs. Bethune was, money was a continual problem. Every donation fed and clothed the children. She lined her thin shoe soles with cardboard and wore second-hand dresses which were restyled in the sewing class.

Considering herself a good beggar, Mrs. Bethune continued to knock on back doors for money. She accepted an occasional racial slur with grace, and sent thank-you notes for every contribution, large or small.

One day, thinking of future generations, she decided it was time to build a permanent school. She found the perfect place, a dumpsite no one else wanted called "Hell's Hole." The owner agreed to take "five dollars down" with the balance of $250 payable within two years.

From sweet potato pies and ice cream sales she raised the deposit. She mailed letters, spoke in churches, hotels, and before the Chamber of Commerce. A believer in integration, she searched for both black and white members for her board of trustees.

One of her letters reached James H. Gamble, founder of the Procter and Gamble soap company. When they met,

All classes at Daytona were practical.
Here, students in a sewing class use
their newly learned skills.

her ebony skin surprised him. But when she spoke about her plans for a science laboratory and a library, her energy and glow attracted him. The next day, after watching her teach, he asked, "Where is this school of which you wish me to be a trustee?"

"In my mind and soul," she said proudly. Gamble immediately scribbled a check for $250 and agreed to be her first trustee. He then persuaded other businessmen to join her board.

For months neighbors and children cleared swampy, mosquito-infested land and planted shrubs and flowers. Laborers laid the foundation for Faith Hall, named for a building at Scotia. Construction proceeded slowly—only progressing when money and supplies were available and men could spare time away from regular jobs.

Finally in October 1907, teachers and students moved into an unfinished, four-story wooden building. Years later a fireproof structure would replace the building.

Soon after, in a field across from The Hall, Mrs. Bethune introduced her girls to gardening. With the help of Frank Taylor, their one hired man, they grew strawberries, sugar cane, and vegetables for school use and for sale on roadside stands to Daytona housewives.

One day Thomas H. White, founder of White Sewing Machine Company in Cleveland, Ohio, arrived unexpectedly in a chauffeured auto. He had enjoyed a student concert and wanted to see Faith Hall. Walking through the building, he observed the unplastered walls, the girls' immaculate mats on dirt floors, the almost empty cornmeal barrel, and a broken Singer sewing machine. He was touched.

The next day and for weeks thereafter, he reappeared, bringing an architect, workers, linens and blankets, a coat for Mrs. Bethune, and a new White sewing machine. He paid for the completion of the Hall and for the installation of bathrooms and plumbing. "I've never invested a dollar that has brought greater returns," he said afterward.

When he died, he left the school a trust fund of $67,000. And Mrs. Bethune named a new dormitory, White Hall, for the school's generous friend.

In 1907, Mrs. Bethune discovered a local turpentine camp where *chippers*, living in hovels, collected turpentine from pine trees. Angry with Daytona city officials for permitting such conditions, she returned with scrub brushes, medicines, slates, first-grade readers, and her Bible. She showed her older girls how to teach cleanliness and child care, and set up the Tomoka Mission School. Within five years, she established schools in four more camps where adults regained their self-respect.

That same year, Mrs. Bethune arranged for her mother to visit the school. Patsy strolled through the building and gardens. She listened to youngsters sing songs she had sung as a slave. She heard her daughter speak before four hundred people, and marveled. How far her child had come!

Left: Mary McLeod Bethune walks the campus of Bethune-Cookman College. She was once listed as one of the fifty greatest women America had produced. Bottom: Mrs. Bethune (right), at the Tomoka Mission School.

When school enrollment reached four hundred, Mrs. Bethune put her first paid teacher, Mrs. Frances Keyser, in charge of teachers and the curriculum. A widow, Mrs. Keyser had been the first black woman to graduate from Hunter College in New York City. Because she seemed to know everything, students affectionately called her their "Walking Encyclopedia."

Mrs. Bethune believed in keeping tuition low and achievement high. Determined to provide quality education, she added high school studies and two years of college courses as students matured.

Whenever teachers and students spied Mrs. Bethune coming through the halls dressed in white, they scurried to tidy their rooms. Ever an educator, she often tacked up messages. A favorite was "Think." She also wrote: "Cease to be a drudge. Seek to become an artist." She believed "There is no menial work, only menial self-esteem."

She always wanted the best for students. In her chapel talks she liked to repeat "You can do anything you want to do, if you put your mind to it. Be what you want to be!"

When she enrolled a few boys in 1908, she changed the institute's name to the Daytona Education and Industrial School. In 1923 she became foster mother to Edward Rodriquez, a teenage dropout who worked in her son's drugstore. With her support, he returned to school. A year later she brought his sister Irma and brother Oliver to the

*Bethune's well-known "Think" sign hangs
over the door to her office.*

school. Irma became a teacher. Oliver became a Daytona policeman, and Edward taught on campus for forty-six years.

Mary Bethune believed every problem held a solution. When a student was stricken with acute *appendicitis*, she convinced a reluctant doctor to operate. But when the girl was segregated on a drafty back porch in the white hospital, she decided African-Americans would have a hospital of their own.

Again she solicited friends for $5,000 to purchase a little cottage behind the school. Andrew Carnegie, the multi-millionaire supporter of public education and libraries, gave the last $1,000. And McLeod Hospital, named to honor her parents, opened with two beds, staffed with the only black doctor in town. She wrote that it grew over the years "into a fully equipped twenty-bed hospital—our college infirmary and a refuge for the needy throughout the state . . . staffed by white and black physicians and by our student nurses . . . until to ease our financial burden, the city took it over."

During the *influenza* epidemic of 1918, which killed some twenty million people worldwide, the hospital overflowed with patients. Nurses even attended patients lying on cots in the school auditorium. Daytona citizens praised Mrs. Bethune and her staff for their professional efficiency. The compliments felt good, but Mrs. Bethune knew more challenges lay ahead.

4

A POLITICAL WOMAN

Unusual as it may seem today, before 1920 American women could not vote. Mrs. Bethune agreed with the black *abolitionist* Fredrick Douglass, who wrote: "Freedom begins at the ballot box." Yet, although Congress had passed the Nineteenth Amendment (which gave women the vote), many Southern states restricted men and women's voting rights. Voters either had to be property owners or have a white sponsor. Several Southern states also collected a poll tax from voters.

Thus, Mrs. Bethune knew she had angered the Ku Klux Klan when she taught adults how to register to vote and how to pass Florida's difficult literacy test. Nonetheless she encouraged them to walk unafraid. "Eat your bread without butter, but pay your poll tax," she advised. And one hundred of Daytona's black citizens did.

She was not surprised when Klansmen paraded past

This old political cartoon makes the point that those Americans who tried to keep black citizens from voting were themselves often poorly educated.

the school while she was out of town. Or when, on election eve, hidden in darkness because the Klan had turned off the street lights, seventy-five men rode again. Encircling the school on horseback in their white, hooded robes, they waved lighted torches, blew shrill horns, and carried a burning cross.

Standing outside as the men approached, Mrs. Bethune ordered all inside lights turned off and every outside light beamed on *them*. "Let them know we're home!" she shouted.

Frightened, girls screamed until one voice, then others, began to sing. "Be not dismayed what e'er betide, God will take care of us!" The masked men disappeared, leaving them unharmed.

The next morning she was at the polls at eight o'clock. Later she wrote: "They kept us waiting [on line] all day but WE VOTED!" Those votes helped defeat the Klan's candidate. Her stand against the Klan brought invitations to speak at black colleges and conferences, where she mingled with poets, artists, writers, and scholars.

Despite the dangers, wherever she traveled she influenced change. Early in the 1900s she joined black womens' organizations to fight lynchings and segregation and to work for children's welfare. She was president of the Federation of Colored Women (1917), and was on the executive board of the National Urban League (1920). She was president of the National Association of Colored Women (1924) and vice-president (1940) of the National Association for the Advancement of Colored People (NAACP). In 1935 she founded the National Council of Black Women, which united 800,000 women nationwide. Eventually she induced department-store owner Marshall Field III to write a check for $10,000, which helped buy the Council's headquarters in Washington, D.C.

Seeking financial security, in 1925 she united her school with Cookman Institute, a Methodist Church school for boys. This merger brought six hundred students and thirty-two teachers into Bethune-Cookman College, with Mrs. Bethune as president.

In 1927, admiring friends sent her on her first vacation. During a four-month tour of seven countries, she met the mayor of London. She drank tea in Scotland with Lady Edith McLeod, a distant relative of her father's ex-master. She met Pope Pius XI in Rome, and African scholars in Paris. She climbed Swiss hills with a cane. In later years she collected canes, which she used for support.

After seeing her first black rose in Switzerland, she sent home two dozen cuttings. She told friends, "A white rose does not want to be red. Every rose wants to be itself. Every person, every nation deserves the right . . . to flourish as itself." A black rose became her trademark.

Back home, she attended a luncheon for the National Council of American Women in the governor's mansion in New York. As the only black present, she paused in the

Mary McLeod Bethune, in later years,
pictured here with one of her canes

doorway until Mrs. Sara Roosevelt, Governor Franklin Delano Roosevelt's mother, led her to a seat of honor next to Mrs. Eleanor Roosevelt, the governor's wife. The friendship begun at that table lasted throughout their lifetimes.

Between 1928 and 1941, Mrs. Bethune's services were in constant demand. During a disastrous Florida hurricane in 1928, the Red Cross relied on her to organize relief for its victims. She served as adviser to presidents Calvin Coolidge and Herbert Hoover, and joined Hoover's commissions on child welfare, home building, and home ownership.

Mrs. Bethune met Mary Crissman for the first and last time at a National Association of Negro Women convention in 1930. Honoring her *benefactor*, she told delegates in Oakland, California, "Invest in a human soul. It might be a diamond in the rough." She would forever be grateful to the woman who paid for her education.

America prospered in the 1920s. In 1929, the stock market collapsed and the country was swept into the *Great Depression*. Unemployment, hunger, and evictions happened everywhere. But the South's poor and youth were hit hardest.

Threatened by creditors when the Depression hit, Mrs. Bethune asked four boys in high school to miss a year of school. This quartet, which included Edward Rodriquez, traveled with her across the country. They sang in

Carnegie Hall and New England Methodist churches. They raised $15,000, which paid the school's debt.

When Franklin D. Roosevelt (FDR) was elected president in 1932, Mrs. Bethune, then a registered Republican, waited to see what this Democrat would do.

Early in his presidency, Roosevelt introduced his New Deal. Pulling the nation forward, he set up programs that put people to work building roads, bridges, post offices, schools, and hospitals, and also established projects in the arts. Segregation continued, but African-Americans, too, rejoined the work force.

Still, five million youths, aged sixteen to twenty-four, were jobless. Juvenile delinquency was rising. To relieve these problems, FDR created the National Youth Administration (NYA) with Aubrey Williams as director and Mrs. Bethune a member of its advisory board.

After a bumbling year, reporting for fourteen million black Americans, Mrs. Bethune told FDR: "The fifteen or twenty dollar checks each month mean real salvation for thousands. We want . . . to open doors for millions." The president promised to help and kept his word.

Weeks later he created a separate department within the NYA—the Office of Minority Affairs—and asked Mrs. Bethune to direct it. Knowing she would be the first black woman ever to hold a federal post, she took the job. In making history, she expected more women to be hired after her.

Mrs. Bethune spent eight years with the NYA. She received several medals and honorary degrees, including the NAACP's prestigious Joel E. Spingarn gold medal. In accepting this medal for her extraordinary achievements, she said, "Unless people have vision, they will perish." And what vision she had!

Then in her sixties, in Washington, D.C., she surrounded herself with energetic young workers who called her "Mother." Wanting the world to know "God made no mistake in making black people," she found part-time jobs for youths so they could stay in school. She started NYA programs in black colleges, including the pilot training project at Tuskegee.

To unite the black specialists in various federal agencies, she held weekly meetings in her apartment. Soon the group of respected advisers to high-ranking officials became known as Roosevelt's "Black Cabinet." With Mrs. Bethune, they organized a Civil Liberties conference, and President Roosevelt passed their recommendations to the 75th Congress.

When Mrs. Bethune learned that Congress planned to cut $100,000 from NYA programs, she rushed to FDR's office. Shaking a finger at him, she pleaded that he not deprive black citizens of their potential leaders. Then, horrified at her outburst, she quickly apologized. Congress approved the budget without cuts the next week.

Conscientiously she read a thousand letters a week.

Mrs. Bethune visits a site as director
of the Office of Minority Affairs.
She worked primarily to enrich the
lives of children and young people.

One year she traveled 35,000 miles to sixty-nine centers in twenty states. Everywhere she upset rules. She never rode freight elevators or entered offices through side doors. In trains she "accidentally" sat in cars reserved for whites. In cabs, she lectured drivers about black history when they tried to avoid black passengers.

Proudly, she witnessed FDR's second inauguration on January 20, 1937. She believed her presence helped make it easier for people to accept African-Americans in high social places.

After Mrs. Bethune became Daytona's first black city official in 1938, she obtained government funds, with Eleanor Roosevelt's help, for a city housing project. But she insisted on NYA-ers building "Pine Haven" and that it include shelter for blacks. And it did.

That same year forward-thinking Americans held the first interracial Conference for Human Welfare in Birmingham, Alabama. To avoid trouble, delegates agreed to separate seating arrangements. But Mrs. Roosevelt changed that. Unexpectedly, Mrs. Roosevelt and Mrs. Bethune met at the entrance. Deeply engrossed in conversation, the women walked down the main aisle and sat together. A policeman politely told the First Lady she had to move. So Mrs. Roosevelt edged her seat to the center of the aisle, and the chairperson opened the meeting.

Under Mrs. Bethune's leadership, NYA programs exceeded all expectations. Over 400,000 youths helped construct

*Eleanor Roosevelt (right) and Mary Bethune
became lifelong friends. Both women
worked hard to improve opportunities
for the underprivileged.*

buildings and beautify the countryside. More than 150,000 men and women were graduated from high school; 60,000 more went to college, and 375 NYA-ers were graduated from college with honors in 1939.

But, the years of hard work took their toll. In 1940, Mrs. Bethune's doctors ordered her to lose weight. She carried 190 pounds on her five-foot-six-inch frame, and because of her *asthma* she needed a *sinus* operation. When she checked into Johns Hopkins Hospital in Baltimore, Maryland, Mrs. Roosevelt sent flowers twice a week. Mrs. Bethune held meetings at her bedside. When she discovered the hospital staff was all white, she insisted on having two black doctors observe her operation. Thereafter, Johns Hopkins' staff included black doctors.

Forever a fighter for justice and equality, Mrs. Bethune never lost an opportunity to break the color barrier.

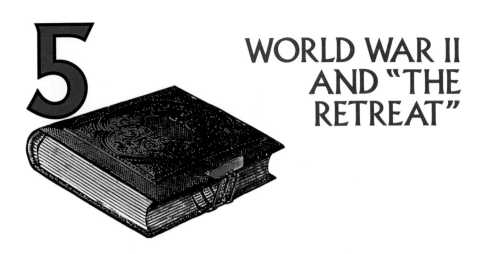

5 WORLD WAR II AND "THE RETREAT"

Once she recovered, Mrs. Bethune worried about world affairs. In Europe, Germany had crossed borders, rapidly conquering unprepared countries. Great Britain was fighting for its life.

Though not yet at war, the United States began to tool up its factories to supply planes, ships, and weapons to England. Skilled blacks *migrated* for better jobs in the factory cities—Detroit, Chicago, New York, and San Francisco. But they found themselves locked out of the defense plants.

Asa Philip Randolph, a Cookman graduate and founder of the Brotherhood of Sleeping Car Porters, mobilized 100,000 men and women for a march on Washington. Mrs. Bethune and other prominent African-Americans supported him.

President Roosevelt knew their cause was just, but felt

the march would endanger the nation. So he signed Executive Order 8802, the law that abolished discrimination in industry and government. Six months later, on December 7, 1941, Japan attacked Pearl Harbor and the United States entered the war.

After Mrs. Bethune's doctors warned her to slow down, at age sixty-five she resigned the presidency of her beloved college and put her energy into the war effort. Serving on several boards, she sold bonds, campaigned for blood donors, worked in *canteens*, visited the wounded in hospitals, and wrote letters to service people. Thousands of soldiers made her their pinup girl.

When Congress created the Women's Army Corps (WAC) in 1942, Mrs. Bethune was appointed assistant director. With segregation an accepted fact of life in the Armed Forces until 1948, the WACs separated black and white women. Nevertheless, Mrs. Bethune worked hard to ensure equality for all service women. She also helped select black candidates for WAC officer training.

Toward the end of World War II, President Roosevelt set plans in motion for a postwar united world. Mrs. Bethune was the only black female official among fifty delegates invited to help write the United Nations (UN) charter.

Unexpectedly, tragedy struck the country when President Roosevelt died on April 12, 1945. Mrs. Bethune flew to Washington, D.C., for his funeral, then on to the first UN meeting in San Francisco. Although no longer physi-

*In July 1942, Mrs. Bethune discusses the
training of black women auxiliaries
at Fort Des Moines.*

cally strong, she spoke at universities, on panels, and in meetings. The charter, translated into five languages, was signed two months after FDR's death, on June 26, 1945. Soon after, Mrs. Roosevelt sent Mrs. Bethune the President's monogrammed walking stick as a gift of their friendship.

After the war, Mrs. Bethune fought for human rights. She wrote a column for three newspapers and worked in many wide-reaching groups, including Planned Parenthood, Association of American Colleges, Association for Study of Negro Life and History, National Sharecroppers Fund, Hadassah (Women's *Zionist* Organization), League of Women Voters, and the American Committee for Yugoslavian Relief.

Her speech favoring American-Soviet friendship (the USSR had been an American ally during World War II) caused problems. Rumors spread that the NYA (since dissolved) had been a Communist front. But when the Committee on Un-American Activities could find no evidence, they had to clear her name.

Mrs. Bethune returned to The Retreat, which was her modest home on the Bethune-Cookman campus. There she entertained friends, students, and visitors who sought her advice. She enjoyed the company of her son, grandson, and six great-grandchildren.

She received Haiti's Medal of Honor and Merit; and President Harry S. Truman appointed her to the Commit-

President Harry Truman signs a bill proclaiming February 1 as "National Freedom Day." On this day the Thirteenth Amendment to the Constitution, which banned slavery, became law in 1865. As president of the Federal Council of Negro Women of America, Mary McLeod Bethune (standing, third from left) was invited to witness the event.

tee of National Defense. At his request, she represented the United States at the inauguration of Liberia's president. Thus, in 1953, at age seventy-eight, she finally walked on African soil.

On May 17, 1954, Mrs. Bethune joyfully learned that the U.S. Supreme Court had declared school segregation unconstitutional. Almost to the day one year later, on May 18, 1955, she died and was buried on her beloved school campus.

On the ninety-ninth anniversary of her birth, a bronze statue created by Robert Berk was unveiled in Lincoln Park, in Washington, D.C., in celebration of her leadership. Inscribed with her legacy, it reads:

I leave you love. I leave you hope. I leave you the challenge of developing confidence in one another. I leave you a thirst for education. I leave you a respect for the use of power. I leave you faith. I leave you racial dignity. I leave you a desire to live harmoniously with your fellow men. I leave you, finally, a responsibility to our young people.

One hundred and ten years after her birth, her portrait appeared on a postage stamp in the Black Heritage Series.

Mary McLeod Bethune, a woman who never said *never*, walked boldly through dangerous events, creating miracles for people everywhere.

Two children play around the statue of Mary McLeod Bethune in Washington, D.C.—the first statue to honor an African-American woman in the United States.

APPENDIX:
SWEET POTATO PIE RECIPE

Mrs. Bethune's recipe is long gone, but there are dozens of other recipes available. This recipe, which was child-tested, is easy to make and tastes delicious. Try it and you will please your family and friends.

3 large eggs
³/₄ cup sugar—half brown,
    half white sugar
Dash of salt
1 teaspoon cinnamon
¹/₂ teaspoon ginger
¹/₂ teaspoon allspice
    (optional)
1 10-ounce unbaked deep
    pie shell

¹/₄ cup orange juice,
    (optional)
¹/₄ teaspoon powdered
    nutmeg
¹/₂ teaspoon ground cloves
1 cup half & half
2 cups *baked* sweet
    potatoes or yams
4 ounces (1 stick) butter or
    margarine

1. Beat eggs until they are foamy. Add sugar, salt, and spices; mix thoroughly.
2. Add half & half and stir. Set aside.
3. Peel and mash baked potatoes. (Yams give the recipe a sweeter taste.) Add the orange juice if you want a lighter pie.
4. Cut the butter or margarine into tiny pieces and add to the mashed potatoes.

58

5. Add the potatoes to the eggs, sugar, cream, and spices. Mix everything thoroughly. Turn mixture into the pie shell and bake in a preheated oven, for ten minutes at 450° F, then for 35 or 40 minutes at 350° F or until the pie is firm.

The pie will serve 8 to 10 people. Enjoy.

GLOSSARY

Abolitionist   one who opposed slavery and worked to destroy it

Appendicitis   inflammation of a narrow tube in the lower right-hand side of the abdomen

Asthma   a condition marked by difficult breathing accompanied by wheezing and a feeling of constriction in the chest

Bale   large bundle of tightly packed merchandise, bound and usually wrapped

Benefactor   one who gives a gift

Canteen   an informal recreation center started by civilians during World War II for members of the armed forces

Chippers   persons who broke off small pieces of trees with an ax, chisel, or edged tool to obtain the tree's sap, or turpentine

Cotton gin   a machine that cleans the seeds, hulls, and weeds from cotton

Great Depression   a period of American history that started in 1929 and lasted until the late 1930s when businesses failed, banks closed, and millions of people were unemployed

Grits   ground hominy; hulled corn kernels

Husking   removing outer coverings of corn, often done at a gathering of farm families and called a "husking bee"

Illiterate   unable to read or write

Influenza   commonly known as the flu; an acute, contagious disease that affects the respiratory system

Jim Crow   an expression referring to any laws or practices used to discriminate against or segregate black people

Lithe   easy flexibility and grace

Lynching   putting someone to death by mob action without following the law or using the legal system

Migrated   moved from one locality to another

Segregation   restriction or separation of people by group or race

Shanties   crudely built dwellings, usually made of wood

Sinus   a hollow cavity in a bone of the skull which receives air through the nostrils

Slate   a small chalkboard students carried to school before notebooks were used

Staples   products having widespread or constant use, such as flour in baking, salt, and potatoes

Surname   the last name of members of the same family

Taffy   a candy, usually of boiled molasses or brown sugar, pulled into shape until hard and light in color

Tenement   an apartment building having minimum standards of safety and sanitation, usually housing poor families

Trough   a long narrow tub filled with water

Underground   a group organized in secrecy to maintain communication and to resist those in power

Zionist   one who promotes the return of the Jews to the land of Israel

FOR FURTHER READING

Bethune, Mary McLeod. "My Secret Talks With FDR," *Ebony*, April 1949.

Halasa, Malu. *Mary McLeod Bethune*. New York: Chelsea House, 1989.

Hicks, Florence. *Mary McLeod Bethune, Her Own Words of Inspiration*. Washington, D. C.: Nuclassics and Science Publishing Co., 1975.

Holt, Rackman. *Mary McLeod Bethune: A Biography*. New York: Doubleday, 1964.

Lerner, Gerda. *Black Women in White America: Mary McLeod Bethune—A College on a Garbage Heap*. New York: Vintage/Random, 1973.

McKissack, Pat. *Mary McLeod Bethune*. Chicago: Childrens Press, 1985.

Meltzer, Milton. *Mary McLeod Bethune: Voice of Hope*. New York: Viking, 1987.

Peare, Catherine Owen. *Mary McLeod Bethune*. New York: Vanguard Press, 1951.

Stern, Emma. *Mary McLeod Bethune*. New York: Knopf, 1957.

INDEX

Kindell Institute, 23
Ku Klux Klan, 27, 39–41

League of Women Voters, 54

McLeod, Edith, 42
McLeod, Mary Jane. *See* Bethune,
  Mary Jane McLeod
McLeod, Patsy, 9–11, 13, 15, 17, 34
McLeod, Samuel, 7, 9–10, 13–14,
  17
McLeod, Sophia, 11, 12
McLeod Hospital, 38
Mayesville Institute, 16
Money raising, 27–28, 30, 31–34,
  42, 44–45
Moody Bible Institute, 21

National Association for the
  Advancement of Colored People
  (NAACP), 42, 46
National Association of Colored
  Women, 41
National Council of American
  Women, 42
National Council of Black Women,
  42
National Sharecroppers Fund, 54
National Urban League, 41
National Youth Administration
  (NYA), 45–50

Office of Minority Affairs, 45

"Pine Haven" housing project,
  Daytona Beach, Florida, 48
Pius XI, Pope, 42
Planned Parenthood, 54

Presbyterian Mission Board, 21–23
Procter and Gamble, 31

Randolph, Asa Philip, 51
Religion, 12–13, 30
Rockefeller, John D., 31
Rodriquez, Edward, 36–38, 44
Rodriquez, Irma, 36–38
Rodriquez, Oliver, 36–38
Roosevelt, Eleanor, 44, 48, 50, 54
Roosevelt, Franklin Delano, 44, 45,
  51–54
Roosevelt, Sara, 44

Scotia Seminary, 17, 19–21
Segregation laws, 25, 30
Sharecropping, 13
Slavery, 9–10

Taylor, Frank, 33
Tomoka Mission School, 34
Truman, Harry S., 54
Tuskegee Institute, 46

United Nations charter, 52–54

Warren, Lena, 28
Warren, Lucille, 28
Warren Ruth, 28
Warren, Susie, 27
White, Thomas H., 33–34
White Sewing Machine Company, 33
Williams, Aubrey, 45
Williams, John H., 27
Wilson, Emma, 16, 17, 23
Women's Army Corps (WAC), 52

Voting rights, 39–41